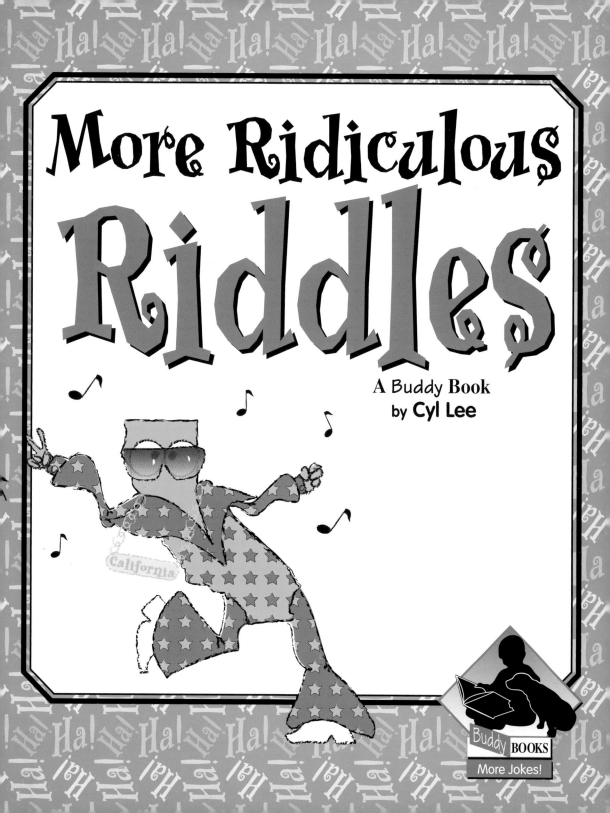

VISIT US AT
www.abdopub.com

Published by ABDO Publishing Company, 4940 Viking Drive, Suite 622, Edina, Minnesota 55435.
Copyright © 2005 by Abdo Consulting Group, Inc. International copyrights reserved in all countries. No
part of this book may be reproduced in any form without written permission from the publisher.

Printed in the United States.

Edited by: Sarah Tieck
Contributing Editors: Jeff Lorge, Michael P. Goecke
Graphic Design: Deborah Coldiron
Illustrations by: Deborah Coldiron and Maria Hosley

Library of Congress Cataloging-in-Publication Data

Lee, Cyl, 1970-
    More ridiculous riddles / Cyl Lee.
        p. cm. — (More jokes!)
    Includes index.
    ISBN 1-59197-876-9
        1. Riddles, Juvenile. I. Title. II. Series.

PN6371.5.L416 2005
818'.602—dc22

                                                                        2004055449

Where do mermaids go to
see movies?

On the way to a water hole, a zebra met six giraffes. Each giraffe had three monkeys hanging from its neck. Each monkey had two birds on its tail. How many animals were going to the water hole?

One, the zebra. All the rest were coming back from the hole!

What word allows you to take
away two letters and get one?

Alone!

What is said like one letter, written
with three letters,
and belongs to all animals?

Eye!

What has one foot and four legs?

A bed!

What flies when it's on and floats
when it's off?

A feather!

What has two arms, two wings, two tails, three heads, three bodies, and eight legs?

A man on a horse who is holding a chicken!

Who invented the first airplane that didn't fly?

The Wrong Brothers!

A man and his dog were going down the street. The man rode, Yet walked. What was the dog's name?

Yeti!

What comes from a tree and fights cavities?

A toothpick!

What can't you see that is always in front of you?

The future!

What's the best parting gift?

A comb!

What is neither inside a house nor outside a house, but no house would be complete without it?

A window!

What is brought to the table and cut, but never eaten?

A deck of cards!

How can you leave a room with two legs and return with six legs?

Bring a chair back with you!

What doesn't exist but has a name?

Nothing!

How do you get down from an
elephant?

You don't get down from an elephant,
you get down from a duck!

11

There is a secret holiday message in the following letters. Can you find it?

No L (Noel)!

Can you spell a pretty girl with two letters?

QT (Cutie!)

Can you spell 80 with two letters?

AT (Eighty!)

How can you spell chilly with two letters?

IC (Icy)!

When is it correct to say, "I is"?

"I is the letter after H!"

What fly has laryngitis?

A hoarse fly!

The more you crack it, the more people like you. What is it?

A smile!

When is it good to lose your temper?

When you have a bad one!

Why do you always find something in the last place you look?

Because when you find it, you stop looking!

What is the first thing ghosts do
when they get in a car?

They boo-ckle up!

How do you change a pumpkin into another vegetable?

You throw it up in the air and it comes down—SQUASH!

What kind of tea helps you feel brave?

Safe-tea!

What can you hold without your hands?

Your breath!

What is very light but can't be lifted?

A bubble!

What can be broken with one word?

Silence!

Some ducks were walking down a path. There was a duck in front of two ducks, a duck behind two ducks, and a duck between two ducks. How many ducks were there in all?

Three ducks, waddling single file!

Where do people go dancing
in California?

What did the blanket say to the bed?

You are undercover!

What dress does everyone have but no one wears?

An ad-dress!

On what nuts can pictures hang?

Wall-nuts!

What is at the end of everything?

The letter G!

How can you make seven even?

Take away the letter S!

What is the quickest way to double your money?

Fold it in half!

If you have $1 million and give away one quarter, and then another quarter, and then another quarter, how much do you have left?

$1 million minus 75¢!

What is the best thing to take into the desert?

Web Sites

Visit ABDO Publishing Company on the World Wide Web. Joke Web sites for children are featured on our Book Links page. These links are monitored and updated to provide the silliest information available.

www.abdopub.com